THE ENCYCLOPEDIA OF SELLING CARS

From the author of *Insider Trading*

TED LINDSAY WITH LARRY BUSH

Bloomington, IN Milton Keynes, UK

authorHOUSE®

AuthorHouse™
1663 Liberty Drive, Suite 200
Bloomington, IN 47403
www.authorhouse.com
Phone: 1-800-839-8640

AuthorHouse™ UK Ltd.
500 Avebury Boulevard
Central Milton Keynes, MK9 2BE
www.authorhouse.co.uk
Phone: 08001974150

First published by AuthorHouse 4/27/2007

ISBN: 978-1-4343-1161-0 (e)
ISBN: 978-1-4343-1162-7 (sc)
ISBN: 978-1-4343-1160-3 (hc)

Library of Congress Control Number: 2007903118

Printed in the United States of America
Bloomington, Indiana

This book is printed on acid-free paper.

AUTHOR'S DEDICATION

I would like to dedicate this book to all the great salespeople I've learned from over the years. Those who are energized and imaginative in thinking outside the box have always been an inspiration to me.

Thanks to my wife, Carolyn, who has always been my encourager. To my sons, Russell and Andrew, who have forever been my Bigger, Better Reason for my work. And to my mom and dad who gave me the foundation for doing the right thing.

God bless you all,

Ted

THE OTHER AUTHOR'S DEDICATION

Writing a dedication has to be the most difficult part of writing a book. If you don't think so, try it. I'll wait.

See? Read it again. You forgot someone, didn't you? It took a while, too.

I believe it takes a village to raise a child, especially in my case.

So here it goes, my dedication in 30 words.

Thanks to Debbie, my beautiful wife (Love you. Mean it.) and my three great kids in Kimmy, Jamie and Kelly. To all of my teachers, especially my mom and dad.

That only took about an hour to write.

Thanks,

Larry

THE AUTHOR

Author of "Insider Trading" and veteran of 34 years in the automobile industry, Ted Lindsay, brings to the market the much-anticipated "The Encyclopedia of Selling Cars."

Soaking up information and ideas over 34 years is what Ted Lindsay did. Now it comes to you in one reference-style location: How to be an overwhelming success in the car business.

Lindsay's down home approach and step-by-step sales processes are proven.

The application derived from "The Encyclopedia of Selling Cars" is universal in any sales profession. It works on every sale!

Read, learn and enjoy. You are getting lessons from a true professional, Ted Lindsay.

TABLE OF CONTENTS

PREFACE

The automobile industry has a worldwide appeal. Whether in the United States, Europe, South America or the emerging markets of China, India and Russia, the industry provides an endless opportunity for personal success. And, the real beauty of the industry is this: the success is available to everyone.

It's fascinating dealing with big ticket items such as automobiles in volume. The financial rewards you can have are absolutely amazing. Anyone who is motivated can certainly change his or her lifestyle, economic status and have all of the things that were never thought possible.

It really is nothing more than being able to get rich helping others get what they want. You become the scratch for their itch; their need for an automobile or the emotional reward they're looking to attain by purchase of an automobile.

No one has ever been successful selling in the automobile industry looking at what they do as a job. It must be a career, a state of mind and a way of life. No other industry offers such an opportunity to become outstanding, by learning the trade and continually growing and learning, adapting, becoming a standout and gaining tremendous satisfaction in one's career. There really is nothing like it.

PURPOSE

My purpose of writing a book such as this is for it to become an actual training guide – a book of fundamentals that are tried and time tested.

The car business is an industry of lots of tricks. But learning the trade is where the long-term success is attained.

I think back on all of my thirty-four years in the automobile industry and the one fundamental question I've always had in my mind -- and I've been sick I didn't do it – is Why didn't I write it all down? More than 30 years you learn all sorts of things, some through training courses and some through the thousands of customers who walk through the door. And the question remains, Why didn't I write it all down? I wonder how many things I have forgotten that are invaluable. Different ways of encouraging myself, regarding my mind set and the mind set of the customers; different techniques in all areas and key phrases and words that actually make you rich.

Thankfully, I have made <u>some</u> notes over the years and I am passing them onto you.

Success in any venture is a function of desire. If you desire something, you will be successful. However, not I nor anyone else can teach desire. But I can expose you to fundamentals and techniques that will provide the foundation for success. The desire, though, is all up to you. Like learning anything: When the student is ready, the teacher will appear.

I'm also writing this to veteran salespeople and for veteran salespeople. One thing I've noticed in my time in the industry is unwillingness to change among the veterans.

Professional golfer Jack Nicklaus said it best when he remarked, "If you're not getting better, you're getting worse." And I don't remember who said this, but, "If you always do what you've always done, you'll always get what you've always gotten."

My message to you veterans: Be a student, prepare to grow and get better. You'll be planning your success. Why not grow? Why not get better? Well, here we go. A life, a career with amazing income, satisfaction and real self-esteem – with no brain damage.

CHAPTER 1

KNOWING YOUR BUYER

One of the best aspects about being in the car business is selling something people are practically dying to own. People will give up lots of luxuries and lots of necessities, lots of stuff they shouldn't give up, just to have a nice car.

Let me give you an example:

Years ago in Kissimmee, FL, we sold a new truck to a young family – husband, wife and two kids. The husband just got a promotion at work and I guess was celebrating it. There arose a problem in that they needed an extra $500 for the down payment to get financed. My company agreed to loan them the money but needed some sort of collateral to insure payment. My salesman, Archie, went with them to their home to see what they had we could use to secure the loan. They had two TVs, a stereo system and a washer and dryer. They talked it over as a couple and their decision was made – we were told to take the washer and dryer.

Now, look at this picture! Does it make sense? No! So get the point: When someone wants a new car, they want it. You <u>are</u> talking to buyers, each and every one of them.

As you begin to sell, remember you are talking to <u>buyers</u>– people who want the product. And, they are <u>all buyers</u>. If they drove to the lot in a car and they're thinking about trading it, know that they <u>don't want that car</u>, no matter how much they want to brag about it. They don't want it. They want to replace it with something else, that's why they came to see you. And, they're looking to fill some sort of need, whether it's a real need or they're purchasing for the purpose of a celebration. In most instances, they are there to fulfill some sort of an emotional reward gained by purchasing a new car.

Let me explain that last sentence. You know when someone *needs* something. Every once in a while, we all *need* a new washer and dryer. I don't like spending money on those types of appliances. Other than clean clothes, I don't get anything out of the appliance store guys pulling up in my driveway and dropping off the latest and greatest in washers and dryers.

But, let me pull in with a new car and the neighbors will come running. And, if they don't, I'll go get 'em! Tee hee

If someone's car has broken down or it needs repair beyond good sense. Maybe their family has changed, they've had a baby and they need to get rid of their small car. These are all needs. These are people who come to the lot with needs.

On the other hand, there is a celebration or some emotional reward..

There is nothing more American than celebrating with a new car. It might be an anniversary or a birthday. Maybe it is a promotion at work. These are the driving forces that people justify coming to the dealership and buying an automobile.

It is the emotional reward that is the biggest single purpose that people buy automobiles. They <u>want</u> a new car. They <u>want</u> to be taller, sexier, sportier, younger or whatever they are thinking. And driving, whether it be to work or to school or to church or just in their own neighborhood, the thought of their neighbors – particularly *that* neighbor – seeing them in a shiny new automobile is what makes people trade in a perfectly good car for a perfectly good car and spend money doing it.

All of the buyers are just like us – just regular ol' working people wanting to replace an automobile with a different one based on some need or desire.

It is critical to remember when they come into the process they are all scared to some degree. They are scared based on previous experiences or the reputation of the car industry. It is hard to erase negative experiences from anyone's mind, too. Whether they were dealt with rudely, discourteously or a myriad of other unprofessional manners, they remember the experiences.

Also, they are very guarded with the fear of paying too much for a product. Keep in mind, we buy and sell cars all day long. The customer does not. This is not a regular event for most people and they feel as if they are at a disadvantage. As well, they have a fear they're going to pick out the wrong car for them or get talked into the wrong car and be stuck with it.

Generally speaking, they come into the dealership with the fear of being taken advantage of, whether it be the car itself, the money or getting caught up in something that later they find out they wish they hadn't have done. So true!

Simply put, they are afraid of making a mistake. This is something that must be addressed with each and every customer. So listen to them and "read" their motives and concerns.

Most customers come in to look at cars and they already have a plan. Many have made some sort of pact and they know their "good cop, bad cop" roles. Or they have promised one another that no matter what, they are not buying a car until they can go home and talk about it. All of this is because there is a fear of making a mistake.

By the time they get to the dealership, they have already figured out what the car is going to cost them. They believe in their minds it is much simpler than the automobile industry chooses to make it. Here is an example of this: The car they're looking at had a price sticker somewhere on it and it was "X" amount. Two or three years ago, they saw someone selling a car like theirs and it was worth "Y." They have taken those two figures and did the math to come up with how little it is going to cost them.

Every customer wants to talk price and/or value for their trade, as well, each of them has these little one line closes set up to throw us so far off track we're unable to do our job. It's always amazed me how often some of us are thrown off guard by them. Let me explain.

What do I mean by one-line closes?

Here is the scenario: A husband and wife come in and they already know the car they want, the color and how much they want to spend. When the salesperson approaches, they say something like, "We are just looking." Do they really mean they are just looking? No. That is one of the most common one-line closes.

Another one-line close is "We're not buying anything." Let me say this about that. Where would you rather spend an afternoon? At the park with your family? Maybe a movie or at the mall with your family. I think standing on a car lot, talking to people in the car business is Haha not on the list of things to do when you have nothing to do. Of course they are there to buy or else they would not be there.

In the selling business, you cannot take anything personally so these one-line closes are defense mechanisms the customer uses. You are going to be taught how to deal with price (and set it aside) along with how to work with the one-line closes. Can't wait! Tell me more!

When everything is said and done, all customers want are answers and information. They want you to respect their time and all customers believe it should be a very simple and fast process. They do not want to be bothered with car lingo and jargon. They want help and they want it from a professional. And, they want to drive their new automobile home right now.

Let me graphically show you and discuss the entire group of buyers. I call it Reaching and Finding the Mother Lode.

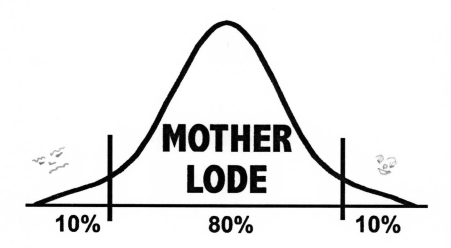

This diagram depicts the total car buying public. The 10 percent on the right are the people who, even on your worst day, you can't stop from getting a new car. You can't insult them or discourage them. They'd buy a car from anyone. Funny thing is this group has been the focus of the entire automobile industry.

The 10 percent on the left is a hardcore group of nasty, miserable people (you know who I am talking about) that you wish you never had met. And, in the outside chance you do sell them, you wish you hadn't. They will continue to make your life as miserable as theirs.

The 80 percent in the middle are just like you and me – they are regular people. They're scared and they want help. But, they require finesse and communication skills to reach them. <u>I'm going to teach you how</u> to reach and find the Mother Lode and I <u>will</u> directly increase your income. You just can't imagine.

CHAPTER ONE

RECAP AND REVIEW

o All customers represent a car deal. At one time or another, they want a new car. They are all buyers.

o They are looking to fill a need or emotional reward.

o They went to a lot of trouble to arrange for the time to come and look. They got the kids settled, or whatever. This time is precious to them and it must be respected.

o Customers have a basic fear of the car industry and those who work in it. And, they are afraid of making a mistake.

o Families who look at cars have a prearranged game plan for shopping.

o They have basically eight reflex objections (one line closes) that you must be able to handle.

o Customers are just regular, decent people who want information, answers and professional help.

o Customers want us to be sensitive to their needs and their time.

CHAPTER 2

YOUR MIND SET

Get this point. Never forget it. Know that it is true and repeat after me: <u>It's always us, it's never them.</u>

What I mean by this is if you took 100 customers who buy automobiles and another 100 customers who buy automobiles, they're all, in reality, the same group of people. It is critical that the salesperson can adapt to each and every one of them. It is not the customer's job to make the salesperson feel comfortable. It is not their job to guide the process. All of that is the salesperson's job. It's always us, it's never them. Until we recognize that fact, we can never reach our highest potential in sales.

Your mind set is critical to whatever success you have in the automobile industry.

The main ingredient to success is <u>your own attitude</u> and we have the opportunity to choose it..

How nice is it that attitude is the most important thing in our lives?

We can't choose how tall we are, how handsome or pretty we are, how short we are or how dynamic we are. We can't choose the color of our hair. We didn't get to choose our parents. We didn't get to choose our brothers and sisters. But we can choose our attitude and the way we look at others and each and every thing that take place in our lives.

In my previous book *Insider Trading*, I covered the next two concepts in more detail. But, they are critical to our mind set and our ability to keep driving ourselves.

The first concept is what I call CAFÉ.

The 'C' in CAFÉ stands for Counting one's blessings. Do that every day. Be happy about your family's welfare, health, the opportunities that are given to me. It's this exercise of counting one's blessings that builds you up and make you feel good. I mean really good – bulletproof. This sets up the 'A' in CAFÉ which is Attitude. How we look at and deal with everything. The Attitude and the opportunity to choose the right one allows us the ability to Focus on the task at hand, which is the 'F' in CAFÉ. And with this opportunity and focusing, it enables one to Execute, the final letter in CAFÉ, our sales process with the utmost efficiency and results.

This mind set technique, when practiced daily, will help make you a powerhouse. As well, because of its positive thinking foundation, it will make you approachable and warm to those with whom you come in contact. Try it – you must!

The other major concept is having a BBR, a Bigger and Better Reason for doing everything.

Selling cars is the hardest business in the world if all you want to do is pay rent or a mortgage or buy food. But the efforts are nothing if the efforts are focused on the accomplishment of a Bigger and Better Reason. Whether it is for one's children, one's family, some major goal, some desire to do something in a big way. But the bigger better reason is what allows one to deal with and respond correctly to adversity because with a BBR, the adversity is not a major roadblock anymore. It is just a bump in the road. It's just part of the day. Why? Because I have a purpose and nothing is going to stop me. I have value and a reason for what I do. I feel great about my noble journey.

Another important concept in the mind set of a successful automobile salesperson is to approach everyone with a servant's heart. That goes for customers and co-workers – everyone. People like to be served. To make it possible, there has to be an understanding of the <u>Principle of Reciprocity</u> in dealing with other people. This principle is simple: if I want a person to like me, I need to like them first. Well really, I need to like myself first. If I want someone to trust me, I need to trust them first. And positioning oneself as a servant, I've found, is the most successful way of transferring this feeling to the customer who is looking for a new car.

My mind set must be that of a professional. Selling cars is not a job; it is a career.

Part of being a professional is having goals, both long and short term. It's critical that these goals are written and are verbally proclaimed by you to another person. This provides a source of accountability that you otherwise can't get. It is like when someone plans to lose weight. If you tell someone you are going to lose a certain amount, it automatically makes you accountable for losing that amount. Because, in the back of your mind, you know there is someone else who knows your plan. That is accountability.

In the car business, you can only manage your own actions and thoughts. You cannot manage the results. And, you live off the byproduct of your actions and your thoughts. You must always stay in a continual mind set of growth – getting a little better every day. When you choose to grow, the hardest step is the first one. But, it takes a lot of first steps.

What makes people great? Attitude. Energy. Focus. Practice. Desire. Determination. You have to believe in your own product, in yourself and in your preparation. Belief has always been the greatest mover of people. The more product knowledge and skills you learn, the better attitude you will have.

Cars can be bought everywhere. Take a look in the newspaper, on the Internet or next to the door as you leave almost any convenience store. Only you can bring the value added to the process. It is the little things you do, the common courtesies — those are what make big things happen.

Statistics show that 75 percent of customers bought because they liked and trusted a particular salesperson. They saw an added value is one person. Always project yourself as a polite, helpful, professional.

Recognize the car business is a sport. It is just like baseball. It's not fair, you work hard, you get good breaks, you get bad breaks. But just like in baseball, you have to play the whole game. Expend all of your energy and leave it on the field. Because, when you go home, the game's over and you have another one tomorrow. *And you have to love on your Sammy + monkey*

This brings to bear that fact that it is very important to your mind set that you maintain balance in your life. Although the car business appears to be fraught with tremendously long hours and hard work, not all of those hours are effective. Time spent with your family will make you more effective at work and help you accomplish the balance and efficiency you are looking for. *Amen!*

Let me share a little idea with you that a pastor of mine gave me many years ago. He and I had many, many chuckles about this very thing. But he taught me about the most important 15 minutes I could spend every day.

"You know," he said, "when you get home from work, Ted, you've been beat up, you've had some successes, you've had some failures. But, now you are coming home and you're worn out. Remember that a man has a biological need to speak 10 or 12 thousand words a day." He continued, "On the other hand, a female has a biological need of speaking 28,000 words a day. When you get home, you've used up you 10 or 12 thousand, but your spouse hasn't."

He said, "You're going to think I'm crazy when I tell you this, but the first thing that comes out of your mouth and what you need to do when you get home is the following. Make sure the television's turned off, and the radio is turned off. Sit down with your wife and ask the open-ended question: How was your day? Then sit there and take it like a man. Well said!

He continued, "The fruits from this conversation are tremendous. It allows your spouse to fulfill more of her biological need to talk. You, on the other hand, become some sort of a mini hero for having offered to spend the time." Plus, this directed, individual time helps to reattach you to your spouse and family. You are not some stranger who works all the time. You are part of a balanced family unit.

The moral to this story is balance helps breed success.

With regard to the actual act of selling cars, remember this: No matter what anyone says, does, implies, writes down, expounds upon or anything to the contrary, remember that everyone who gets sold takes delivery of the new car. And they'll take delivery right now. Remember, too, it's always me, never them who's responsible.

CHAPTER TWO

RECAP AND REVIEW

o   I must be accountable for my own success. It's always us, it's never them.

o   Attitude is everything.

o   I must have a purpose, a BBR.

o   Communication skills will be an endless study.

o   I must present myself with a servant's heart.

o   Goals – both short and long term – are critical.

o   I can only manage my own actions, not the results.

o   I am a work in progress.

o   I must add a value in me to the process.

o   There must be balance in my life.

o   I am responsible for my success.

CHAPTER 3

OPPORTUNITY AND PREPARATION

The greatest thing about the car business is it's the easiest industry in the world to be outstanding.

The industry is full of undertrained, under motivated and underachieving people who have no formal knowledge of how to deal with others. The opportunities are endless.

Look sharp, feel sharp, think sharp. You will be a positive charge to an otherwise negative world.

In order to be prepared, we have to deal with three particular areas that are the foundation for success.

Physical self – No different that any sport, there has to be some degree of physical health. You need to be rested and be in some sort of physical condition so your energy never wanes during the course of a long day. That does not mean you have to run marathons or win triathlons. Just be in shape by going for walks or losing weight. By being in shape, you will also help almost every aspect of your being.

Mental health – Specific to the car business, in order for you to feel good about yourself, you need to know the product. You have to be mentally capable of doing the business functions that are required in our business. You have to know the products inside and out, front wards and backwards. This provides for the greatest self-worth which is important in dealing with the daily bumps and potholes you encounter. There is strength in knowing you have value. *what a large value you have :)*

Emotional **health** – There has to be some substance to us; we have to believe in something. In a business of rejection, you have to be strong enough to learn from all of your experience and keep your emotions on an even keel. There are going to be months where you are the top salesperson in the organization and there will be times where you are not. Either way, your emotional health needs to be steady and unwavering.

If you have those three areas – physical, mental and emotional – healthy, you will be a force to be reckoned with. It will allow you to think, speak and act positively.

As humans, we will always follow our dominant thought. What I mean is this: for some it is a great day, for others that same day is tough. I've always felt grateful to be part of it. "Goodness, gracious it is a wonderful day." At the same time, I've worked with people that every moment, from the time they got to work, was pure drudgery. Whom do you think was more successful?

The dominant thought needs to be positive. So do the words we speak and our actions.

One of the fundamentals of success is staying positive. Another fundamental is to always think about what you know, but talk about

<u>what sells</u>. People are only interested in what's in it for them. The buyer is driven by conversation that highlights what's in it for them as opposed to the raw information.

Listening is the wallet where the money is kept. My dad told me, "Always listen. As you get older in life, you can't help but learn."

The great advantage of listening is you already know what you know, now you're finding out what the other person knows and possibly what drives them. Generous listening is appreciated by customers. They can actually feel and know that you're actually hearing what they're saying and absorbing the information. If you are a successful listener, you'll get compliments and very satisfied customers.

Women have always proven to be the best generous listeners. If you watch two women in conversation, one will be speaking and the other will be nodding, smiling and showing other signs she is *genuinely* listening. She's not nodding in agreement with everything that is being said, she's nodding to show the other person she is listening and that what is being said is important to her. We should all have such a skill!

And for you men who are reading this, have you ever noticed our wives have the skill to make many of their ideas ours? That's generous listening.

Years ago I learned a good lesson from a man I could not close, no matter what.

So true! When you nod to demonstrate listening, it puts the speaker at ease. It's a positive reinforcement tactic my prof. in Columbia used to get me to speak in public :

Then, he shared the story of Johnny's mom. I am still grateful for this story because it taught me about listening, as opposed to hearing. Here is the story of Johnny's mom.

Johnny's mom has three kids. The oldest one is named Penny. The middle one is named Nickle. What is the youngest child's name?

I came back to him with the answer: Dime.

And he said, "Let me give you the story again. Johnny's mom has three kids. The oldest one is named Penny. The middle one is named Nickle. What is the youngest one's name?"

I told him Quarter or Fifty Cents, and he said: "Well, let me share the story with you again. Johnny's mom has three kids. The oldest one's name is Penny. The middle one's name is Nickle. What's the youngest one's name?"

In my frustration, I said, "Hell, I don't know. What is it?" And he said, "Whose mom are we talking about?" I said, "Johnny's mom."

He said, "If you want to sell things, you better learn how to listen." Ha!

Great story and a great lesson for me.

Another area of importance to be successful in car selling business is one simple phrase: <u>They can't beat the teeth</u>. That is, if you bring a smile to work with you every day and be prepared to use that smile, you can't be beat. And boy do you have a killer smile!

Have you ever seen that person on television who just got stabbed by a question and then you see this big grin come over his face for a couple of moments while he collects his thoughts? Don't ever let them see you sweat, just use that smile.

Quality questions will become one of the keys to your success. The size of your pocketbook is directly proportional to the quality of questions you ask. I'm going to teach you some quality questions later in this book.

Every salesperson should have what I call an Evidence Manual with them at all times. You can think of it as a resume, but it is more than just the highlights of a career. It is a notebook or binder that has some information about products and the dealership. But, most importantly, it is something you can show the customer that is a history of you. It should have a biography of you, pictures, family pictures, awards, accolades, good letters from customers, bad (but not too bad) letters from customers and blank copies of a Customer Service Evaluation.

CUSTOMER SERVICE EVALUATION
<u>YOU ARE IMPORTANT TO ME!</u>

Feedback allows me to build a better business atmosphere.

Please help me. I appreciate your consideration.

Please list any FAVORABLE impressions or THINGS I DID RIGHT!

_____

_____

_____

_____

Please list the "STUPIDEST" things I do!

_____

_____

_____

_____

Why we DIDN'T DO BUSINESS TODAY?

_____

_____

_____

_____

You want people to see you as a work in progress as well as an engaged professional.

Finally, in regard to your preparation, prepare yourself to learn and use 'bridge statements.' Those are phrases that will enable you to set one line of thinking and conversation aside and 'bridge' to another. This is a very subtle tool, but the skilled professional uses it effectively in redirecting the conversation while still acknowledging the customers' point of view.

Some examples are:

ACKNOWLEDGMENT	**BRIDGE**
Along with that...	Have you ever considered...
I appreciate what you say...	Although, I one had a client tell me...
What you say makes sense...	Another thought might be..
	What do you think?
Yes, but have you ever thought (or felt)...	Another possibility might be...
I understand how you feel, I once felt like that.	Until I found or discovered...
That's understandable...	By the way...
I understand. I'm confident once I show you...	Fair enough

Work on and practice bridges. Come up with your own and use them to your advantage. This tool will reap tremendous rewards.

On <u>your</u> best day you'll never meet someone you can't sell.

CHAPTER THREE

RECAP AND REVIEW

o   Opportunities in the car business are endless.

o   I must be a positive change.

o   The foundation for success involves my physical self, mental health and emotional health.

o   I will follow my dominate thought.

o   Listening skills are success skills.

o   They can't beat the teeth.

o   The size of my pocketbook is directly proportional to the quality of the questions I ask.

o   I want everyone, particularly customers, to see me as a work in progress.

o   "Bridge phrases" are critical to success.

o   On my best day, I'll never meet someone I can't sell.

CHAPTER 4

HERE'S A QUESTION OR TWO: ARE YOU READY FOR WORK TODAY?

How is your attitude? You might want to use your CAFÉ process. What is your BBR? Are you a positive charge? Are you physically, mentally and emotionally prepared?

Being a positive charge is being an encourager. And that means all of those around you, prospects and associates you encounter and most important, yourself. What is your plan of action?

You can't manage the result. You can only manage your activities or your actions.

How about your network of employees, the one you'll need to get the job done? Do you know all of the employees? Have you spent time to walk around and say "Hello" to everyone?

How much time have you set aside for follow-up calls and mail-outs? What about prospecting referrals? How much time are you going to spend on product training? How much time do you plan to spend working walk-in traffic?

Year after year (for 34 of them to be exact), I've watched grown people come to work in the car business and stand outside and wait for drive-in traffic only. I know this is a crucial part of making a sale, but in all my years, I've never seen a bag of money fall out of the sky and in the arms of one of these guys. Drive-in traffic is part of the job, but there has to be a method.

I believe in professional activity because it results in you having self esteem. Because you are engaged in and part of a noble pursuit, you have worth and value. This self esteem, day in and day out, is critical to your longevity.

I've been asked many times about the shortcuts to success in the automobile industry. Let me address that right now. There are no shortcuts to success. Said like a true Brodlieb ☺

CHAPTER FOUR

RECAP AND REVIEW

o   Checklist for daily success: attitude, CAFÉ, BBR and a positive charge.

o   Prepared physically, mentally and emotionally.

o   Have an action plan and manage it.

o   Stay active.

o   It is easier to happily achieve than it is to achieve being happy.

o   Noble pursuit, self esteem.

CHAPTER 5

PROSPECTING AND PHONE CALLS

The most simple form of prospecting there is has a lot to do with your self-esteem regarding what you do. If you feel good about what you do, you'll be more than happy to let everyone know you're in the car business. You can be at the dry cleaner, drugstore or wherever and you let anyone know you are in the car business – and proud of it. And remember, people want to know someone in the car business.

I have a method that will provide you with a prospect within 60 seconds. That's right, 60 seconds. And it goes like this:

"Excuse me (Sir or Ma'am), if I may, part of my training at ABC Motors is that I complete a number of these short surveys. It only takes a couple of minutes. Would you kindly help me?"

You'll not only have a prospect within the guaranteed 60 seconds, but your interviewing skills will go through the roof. Look over the survey on the next page, then I'll explain.

CONSUMER SURVEY

What make and model of car do you own? _____

How long have you owned it? _____

    Like best? _____

    Like least? _____

What is your normal buying cycle?

    Number of years? _____

    Time of year? _____

    Why? _____

What are the "triggering events" that tell you its time to trade?

    Emotion _____

    Needs_____

    Financial _____

    Other_____

What features are or are not on you current vehicle that you would like to have on you next vehicle?

_____

What do you wish would change about "the buying process?"

Dealerships in general_____

    New Vehicles _____

    Used Vehicles _____

As a consumer, what "causes" loyalty?"

    Car make _____

    Dealership _____

    Salesperson_____

The psychology of the survey is simple. Once you get started you'll find out what the customer likes plus, and more importantly, what drives them. Because it is a survey, gathering this information <u>in the third person</u> becomes more truthful and easier to obtain.

Follow along so you understand the "why" portion of getting the survey completed.

What make and model do you own? <u>Gets you started.</u>

How long have you owned it? <u>New or used buyer, plus what they like and don't like.</u>

NOTE: At this point, make sure everything is being done conversationally, not in the form of playing 20 Questions.

What is you normal buying cycle? <u>Are they ready now? Is there a time of year they usually buy. Why?</u>

What are the triggering events that tell you it's time to trade? <u>Listen, listen, listen. They're giving you clues.</u>

What features that are or are not on your current vehicle would you like to have on your next one? <u>Listen. You might know or have something that would excite them.</u>

What do you wish would change about the buying process? <u>They are telling you HOW to sell them.</u>

As a consumer, what causes loyalty in car makers, dealerships and salespeople? <u>This is very enlightening. Keep probing. You'll learn a lot.</u>

Finally, thank them for helping you and allowing you to take some of their time. Say to them, "I've asked you a lot of questions. Now, do you have any for me?" Then take it from there, wherever it goes. *Brilliant!*

Another source of ready prospects is your current owner base. This includes their birthdays, anniversaries and the birthday of their purchase. Let me explain how critical this is. These are real world statistics.

Ninety percent of the automobile buying population was never contacted after the first month of ownership of their new vehicle. Eighty-two percent of those buyers cannot recall the name of their salesperson one year later. And, most important, 98 percent of all those purchasers will buy another car.

When you think you've got absolutely nothing to do, call your previous customers. Even if it is just to say hello, how are you doing? Whatever the case, stay in contact. When they tell a friend they know someone in the car business, you want them to give your name.

Those single phone calls will reap tremendous rewards. People are impressed when a salesperson calls just to see how they are doing, not trying to sell anything. Believe me when I tell you, the seed will be sown and the harvest will come.

Based on these thoughts of prospecting, it could provide you with a steady flow of customers and income from month to month. That is opposed to the brain damage you will suffer during free time at the dealership and being broke every month or so. Phone calls – they work.

Eighty percent of all people who call an automobile dealership buy within one week. It is very important when handling incoming sales calls to make an impression, because over the telephone, there are only two things that can happen.

First, make an impression and second, set an appointment.

It's important to be brief and work to stay on a task because you can't sell a car over the phone. But, you can sell yourself and you do that by making an impression. Everything you say should be straightforward and be prepared to make their experience fast, easy and simple. They will want <u>your</u> help if you make it seem easy and professional.

By making an impression it enables you to sell the appointment. The appointment can be at their home, business or the dealership. The idea that a customer *has* to come to the dealership is dead and should be buried. When you go to the extra effort and offer to take the vehicle to them, it adds to the impression of professionalism and service.

Here are two thoughts on setting a face-to-face appointment.

One is simply asking the question: "When would you like to drive one?"

Secondly is to let the customer know you feel they have many questions and when would they have the opportunity to come by and you could lay out all of the information for them. That way they could have what they need when they are ready to buy.

The appointment is the critical factor. To arrive at an agreed-upon time, it is easiest to narrow it down by using alternative choices.

"Mrs. (or Mr.) Jones, I have some time available this afternoon as well as between 9:00 and 10:00 a.m. tomorrow. Which would be better for you?" This leads them and yet, lets it be their decision. Remember, their idea is always better than yours. *Its just like teaching Autistic kids!*

After you've set the appointment, offer them your cell number just in case their plans change and they can let you know. That is also the quickest way to get their phone number so you can offer them the same courtesy. Now you have the name, phone number and – most importantly – the appointment. *Easy, right?*

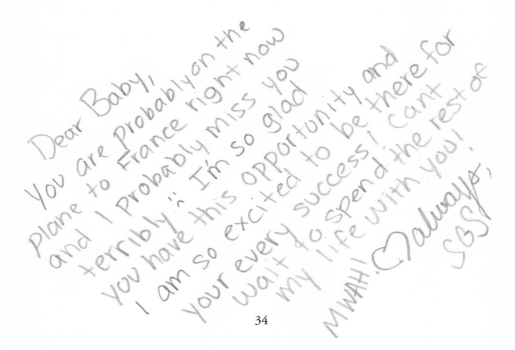

Dear Baby!, You are probably on the plane to France right now and I probably miss you terribly :: I'm so glad you have this opportunity and I am so excited to be there for your every success! I can't wait to spend the rest of my life with you!. MWAH! ♡ always SGS

CHAPTER FIVE

RECAP AND REVIEW

o   Let the world know what you do.

o   Talk to people who might buy a car.

o   Survey your customers.

o   Owner base calls.

o   Prospect a little, not a lot.

o   Incoming phone callers are buyers.

o   Make a positive impression.

o   Sell an appointment.

CHAPTER 6

YOU GOTTA HAVE GOALS AND ACTIVITY MANAGEMENT

Here is a great idea for goals and activity management – plan to get better each day; plan to raise your level of play and professionalism. Activity is the precursor of all success. You cannot manage results, you can only mange your activities.

Here is what I think about goals:

Goals must always be written and verbalized to another human being. This helps with accountability and all of the dynamics related to it. Those who are involved in the dynamics of business are always the winners. Those who are static seldom win.

There are two ways you can set goals. One is a bit more involved. The other is more controlled by you. It really depends on what best appeals to you.

In the first one, you can decide the income goal you want. Divide that by an anticipated dollar per sale gives you the number of sales you need, divided by your percentage of closing or your closing ratio, which gives you the total number of face-to-face prospects you need to talk to. Divide that number by the number of days you work and that gives you the number of face-to-face prospects that you need to engage your activities within each day. Here is an example:

$8,000 Desired income for month

divided by $400 income per sale

= 20 sales needed

100=prospects needed

divided by 20 working days

= 5 prospects talked to per day

The second one, you start your day with the thought and plan that you will call 'X' number of previous customers. You will mail out 'X' number of written contacts and you will talk face-to-face 'X' number of prospects prior to going home.

The second is a tried and true system. If you do this on a daily basis, you will win. Take the number prospects talked to daily times the number of days worked. That equals the total number of prospects. Take that times your closing percentage and that will equal your sales which equal your total income. Here is an example:

Today, I will call ___ previous customers.

Today, I will mail out ___ post cards.

Today, I will work with 5 prospects face-to-face before going home.

5 prospects x 20 days = 100 prospects

multiplied by 20 percent closing ratio

= 20 sales for the month

I prefer the second of the two because it's all management activity related. You take the initiative and manage the action. There is a big difference between doing and hoping.

You should never set your goals too low. In fact, I believe one becomes more successful if he never really reaches his goals. It is kind of like the old Hertz and Avis concept. Avis always tried harder.

Remember, results can't be managed, we can only manage our activity. Activity is the precursor to success.

CHAPTER SIX

RECAP AND REVIEW

o   Must have long term and short term goals.

o   Get a little better every day.

o   Stay active, be dynamic.

o   Have a game plan for each activity.

  – Unsold calls

  – Owner base calls

  – Mailouts

  – Lot time

o   I will accomplish each task.

CHAPTER 7

ON STAGE! FRONT AND CENTER

Getting ready to go on stage should be exciting. And, if you are carrying a lot of energy with you, it will be exciting to those around you. Energy begets energy. If you are around someone who is enthusiastic, it is hard not to be enthusiastic. You have to be internally excited.

I've always felt that the way and speed with which I drove <u>to work</u> and then home <u>from work</u> was a gauge of my energy and enthusiasm.

Have you ever seen the guy that comes in late or always at the last minute? Or picture the one who won't even talk to a prospect if it's near closing time. Successful people are geared and ready to go. I've always gotten to work early and was at full steam when the others arrived. I'd like to add to the old saying that "The early, energized and prepared bird gets the worm."

Monitor you arrival and departure mood. It will tell you where you are, and if you a energized, those around you will be moved by you.

Throughout my thirty-four years in the automobile business, it has been my experience that successful people create a tremendous wake. Have you ever seen a big boat come by and noticed its wake? All of the other little things in the water are just sitting there bobbing and getting caught up in the movement. Successful people create a big wake.

In any field!

Like the wake, selling is about the transference of feelings. If you ask me how business is, I'll tell you each and every time, "It's unbelievable."

Realize that perception is reality. It does not matter what we say or do, it's what is perceived by our clients and those around us that really matters. In the car business, we have two choices. One is to be corny and rich, or cool and poor. We are salespeople. We're show people and corny sells. Energy, enthusiasm, engagement and execution are our life's blood.

When customers arrive on the lot, their perceived value of the product for sale is average or low. On the other end of the graph is the price of the product. At that time, it's higher than their perceived value. This is known as the Price/Value Quotient.

In the car business, we have two opportunities to have this make sense to the customer. We have the choice to either increase the value in their mind or lower the price to match their own perceived value.

Which do you think is best? I know, I know ☺

Stay off the price and stay on value. Dropping the price makes anyone want to shop. They will think to themselves, "Gosh, how cheap can I get it?"

It's important to remember you've got to give everyone a chance to buy a car, regardless of their conversations or one-line closes that try to throw us off track.

And, there is no disgrace in not selling someone a car. However, there is disgrace though in not using all the tools available to giving it your all.

About 80 percent of all major purchases are made by females. Remember that little tid-bit. She holds the purse strings. *You knew that though!*

Make sure you are asking opinions and feelings as much as possible. Quality questions are very important. You want to learn and "feel" what they're saying.

- Give everyone a chance (a whole show) to buy.

- Remember there is a price/value quotient. When prospects arrive the value is always lower than the marked price. You must make the value exceed the price. <u>You must!</u> And, you must stay off talking price. Learn to set the price aside then leave it alone. There is an old saying: "Price drop will make 'em shop."

- More than 80 percent of all purchases are decided by the female – don't leave her out.

- Ask often for the customers' opinions and feelings. You want them to do the talking.

- There is no disgrace in not selling someone. But, there is disgrace in not using all the tools available.

ENERGY! ENTHUSIASM! ENGAGEMENT! EXECUTION!

Here we go!

Repeat after me: On my best day, I can't meet anyone I can't sell.

It's always me, it's never them.

Let's get going!!

Woo hoo!,

Here we go,....

CHAPTER SEVEN

RECAP AND REVIEW

o   Energy begets energy.

o   Internal excitement.

o   I must monitor my mindset.

o   I can be corny and rich, or cool and poor.

o   Value is my friend, see it in everything.

o   Females hold the purse strings.

o   I must get opinions and feelings.

o   Energy, enthusiasm, engagement and execution.

Heres a
monkey kiss!
xxx meow

CHAPTER 8

ENTER THE PROCESS ZONE

The sales process must be fundamentally sound. Keep in mind the Principle of Reciprocity – if I want them to like me, I should like them first. If I want them to have fun, I'd better plan to have fun first. If I want them to be a buyer, I'd better assume they are a buyer. _Love it!_

There are really 10 steps to the sales process and I'll go into them in a minute. That may sound a bit complicated and consuming, but we can make it very simple. As a matter of fact, it can be turned into a one-step process and still have a certain degree of success.

What is that one step process? It's called "make a friend."

By that one simple thought, people will buy a car from you because you haven't said or done anything to upset them. You are a nice person and they've enjoyed themselves. You didn't complicate the matter and did not muddy the water to the point where they couldn't buy.

Help your friends find something they would like to own. Show it to them and ask them to buy it.

Have you ever wondered why so many people who are new to the car business sell a bunch of cars and they really don't know what they are doing? They don't know any better! They approach the customer and are friendly and try to be helpful. They find their new friend something they would like to own. They show it to them, show them what it costs and ask them to buy it. Not a bad thought!

Each and every step in the sales process is critical. Although while we're trying to stay on task, the customer will do their very best to throw us off by saying things and confuse our sequence of the steps. Each step is critical and, for maximum rewards, each prospect must be given completely the "whole show."

On the other hand, customers want this process to be time efficient. They do not want to waste their time and – even more important – they do not want YOU to waste their time.

The 10 Lindsay Steps are:

1. GREETING

2. STATEMENT OF INTENT

3. DISCOVERY

4. SELECTION

5. PRESENTATION

6. DEMONSTRATION

7. THE TRIAL CLOSE

8. THE WRITE-UP

9. THE PRESENTATION OF FIGURES

10. THE CLOSING

Before we discuss each step individually, let's look at them in groups in order to increase your feel for the importance of each one.

CHAPTER EIGHT

RECAP AND REVIEW

o   Principle of reciprocity.

o   Give everyone a chance to buy.

o   I must make a friend.

o   Keep it as simple as possible.

o   My process must be fundamentally sound.

o   Give them the "whole show."

o   Smile and have fun.

CHAPTER 9

MAKING SENSE OF IT ALL

GREETING, STATEMENT OF INTENT, DISCOVERY

These three steps are known as the "If I'm going to sell them a car" steps. They are where we discover the needs and wants of the buyer. We get a feel for them. This is where rapport building that takes place and we start to build friendship and trust.

SELECTION, PRESENTATION, DEMONSTRATION

These steps can be looked at as the "How much I'm going to sell it for" steps. They are the value steps – value vs. price. This is where the profit lies and determines how much I get paid.

TRIAL CLOSE, WRITE-UP, FIGURE PRESENTATION, CLOSING

These are known as the "when" steps. They represent a rapport-value vs. price report card. You get to find out just how good of a job you did. How excited are they?

Each step is critical and interrelated. There are some "truths" in understanding the sale process. Rapport is paramount. People are listened in buying not talked into buying. It's the customers' needs and wants that drive your process – not your desires.

To any prospect, until they understand the value, the price is always going to be too high. Customers pay attention to people they believe have something important to say. Customers <u>must</u> feel your belief if you expect to sway theirs. You must <u>earn</u> the customer's business.

Here is how all of these steps work.

CHAPTER 10

THE GREETING

They can't beat the teeth. The ability to meet and greet a customer is the cornerstone of success in the sales business. The ability to make a stranger in a strange place feel comfortable is an acquired skill. You can do it, but it is going to take practice.

Please note that rapport is going to be critical. With rapport the customer will let you take them completely through the sales process.

Remember, the customer is coming to the dealership's lot with memories of previous experiences which lead to fears, and make them question everything you do. The customer brings this baggage with them when they arrive. It is the salesperson's job to alleviate those fears and feelings.

As a customer is driving up pulling into a parking place, they are making decisions faster than you can count and those decisions are related to everything. It is my hope that the dealership creates a customer-friendly atmosphere. That will help, but the customer is still making decisions.

In one study, it was shown that, in the first 10 seconds upon arriving, customers make seven critical decisions with regard to trustworthiness, integrity and professionalism. Ten seconds, seven critical character decisions.

You need to make your greeting count because you only have one chance to make a first impression. Remember the customer is still making these types of decisions. The customer had better not smell a rat or spot a vulture because, believe me, they will leave as quickly as they arrived.

Just as important as your smile is the way you are dressed, whether your shoes are polished, your posture and how you carry yourself. Customers will also measure social skills with regard to shaking hands and eye contact. It may sound a bit crazy, but it is real! They've decided if we're decent people or not.

Ten seconds, seven critical character decisions. You need to make a favorable impression.

While most dealerships have some sort of preferred greeting, it is all going to be a matter of interpretation and individual personality.

Most important, the customer must be made to feel comfortable in their unfamiliar environment. Some of the ways to make someone feel comfortable (after a good greeting and handshake) is to see if either of them needs to use the restroom. Maybe someone needs a soft drink. These are simple innocent ways of doing something different, something that stands out.

Let's go back to just the fundamental greeting itself: Anyplace you or I ever go in life, we like to be made to feel welcome.

Think about when you go over to a friend's house and how you are greeted. Your friend looks you in the eye, gives you a genuine and comfortable handshake and smiles at you. They might even toss in a "Nice to see you." You feel good.

That is the same feeling customers want and deserve. Smile, posture, how you carry yourself and eye contact. Here is an example:

"Welcome to ABC Motors. My name is Ted Lindsay. And your name, sir?" Usually it is often by a first name, whereby you follow with "And your last name, sir?"

The last name is critical because everyone in the world has a favorite last name and it is their own. Use the last name time and again. After getting that, turn to the lady and say, "And yours, ma'am?" Then comes her response, whereby you follow with, "I'm sure glad you are here." We want their last name. This is a fundamental that comes from the greeting.

It is important that this little social process takes place. You will always sell more cars to "Mr. and Mrs. Wilson" than you will sell to "Joe and Betty." Every single time use their last name. And, don't stop using their last name. Having done so, ask Mr. and Mrs Wilson <u>how you can be most helpful to them.</u>

Immediately you want to fall into the servant role. Hopefully they'll tell you what they want and hopefully you'll listen.

If, for some reason, your customer short cuts you in this area, don't worry. Ask them how they'd prefer to be treated while they are here. At some point you'll be given a direction to go. You need to be patient, listen and follow the lead.

Again offer the cold drink, cup of coffee, use of the bathroom — anything that will increase their comfort level in their new environment.

Keep in mind: the customers all have a game plan. They have a series of what I call One-Line Closes all prepared for us. You have to have an answer for each of them.

Here are the Famous Eight One-Line Closes.

1. "We're just looking"

2. "We're not buying anything today."

3. "This is the first place we've stopped."

4. "We're not buying till next month, but... ."

5. "We only have 10 minutes."

6. "What's your best price on a... ?"

7. "What's my (name of car) worth?"

8. "We're shopping three dealerships and we want your best price."

You just called on how i ♡U!.

Each and every one of these feel like someone throwing a bucket of water on a campfire. In reality, they are only reflex objections stemming from the customer's fundamental fear of buying a car and <u>making a mistake</u>. Think about it for just a second: In reality, who would drive into a dealership when they only have 10 minutes? I don't know about you, but I'd rather sit at a traffic light for 10 minutes than pull into an automobile dealership for 10 minutes.

But, customers will use these all the time and you have to be ready and address each one while setting yourself up to bridge your way to the next discussion.

These reflex objections are just the way the customer sets the stage. When a customer uses one of these lines, they are just telling us they are not ready for us yet. And, we need to respect their space. We're in the process of earning our way into their circle.

Let's look at each one and how to handle them.

"We're just looking" We know they are just looking for a new car. A good response could be, "I understand." That is where it all begins. "Would you care to be left alone a moment or do you have any questions so I might be able to point you in the right direction?"

Ninety percent of the time, your involvement will start right now.

"We're not buying anything today." We know that is a bunch of garbage. They are *looking* to buy a car. You can try to point them in the right direction. "Gosh, is there a type of car you would be interested in? I can show you where they are or I'll point them out to you."

"This is the first place we've stopped." "I'm happy you chose us. What questions do you have that I could assist you with?"

"We're not buying till next month, but... ." You could answer that with something like this: "I would be happy to give you all the information I can today so when you are ready next month or the month after, you'll have everything you need to know." Fair enough.

"We only have 10 minutes." Your response: "OK, folks, I appreciate that. What information could I provide for you in the time you have (don't repeat the time frame) so your time will be well spent?"

"What's your best price on a... ? "I'll be happy to get that for you. Do you want the base price information or are there certain accessories or equipment that's important to you. By the way, what equipment is important to you?' That question usually leads into the process of the sale.

"What's my (name of car) worth?" "Let me get your car professionally appraised for you while we're looking at other automobiles and that will save you some time in the long run." That comment, too, will lead to the sales process.

"We're shopping three dealerships and we want your best price." "Great! I hope the service I provide you will lead you to consider me when you are ready to buy. Now, how can I be most helpful to you?"

Addressing these initial responses, these reflex objections of the customer is critical to making the sale. Think of what can happen from not lending credibility to any of these statements! That is one big reason so few clients in the car business are provided good service and it's why their impression is usually negative.

Our desire is to make a dynamic first impression and make them feel comfortable with the environment. We're on our way to becoming friends and building rapport.

CHAPTER TEN

RECAP AND REVIEW

o   Can't beat the teeth.

o   I must make the customer comfortable in their new environment.

o   Rapport is critical. It allows the process to take place.

o   I must make a great first impression.

o   I'll look sharp, feel sharp and be sharp.

o   No car jargon, no car lingo.

o   I am a servant and I will be helpful.

o   I'm prepared for reflex objections or one line closes.

o   The customer is going to feel so comfortable with me, the will want the whole show.

o   My great first impression will get the ball rolling.

CHAPTER 11

STATEMENT OF INTENT

A Statement of Intent is a tremendously effective tool. You use it at the end of your greeting. The idea with the Statement is to give the customer a degree of comfort by providing them a road map of what you intend to do for them while they are with you.

Remember, fear and price are the two biggest issues on their mind. There is the fear of how they're going to be treated and/or making a wrong decision. And then there is price. Everyone from their pharmacist to their dry cleaner to their next-door neighbor all the way to their uncle who used to work in Detroit has told them how to buy a car and get the best price.

To stand out in the business, give your customers a road map that will provide them a comfort level and help alleviate those fears. You will win over and over again.

Here is a Statement of Intent I use. You can adapt it and make it more 'you' but make sure you keep the idea alive.

"Mr. and Mrs. Wilson, my name is Ted Lindsay. I've been at ABC Motors for 'X' number of years and I absolutely love what I do. What I would like to do, if it is all right with you, is help you find a car that's perfect for you and your family. Then I will go over it with you so you will understand what does what. Then we'll drive it. When we are done with that, I'll lay out all of the price and payment information for you so when you are ready to buy, you'll have all the facts. Fair enough?" "Fair enough."

The reason for this Statement is that you need to make sure the customer has a comfort level with what is happening throughout the entire sales process.

Let me back this up with a real world example we can all relate to: Going to the doctor's office.

How many times when we all go to the doctor's office, we go up to a little glass window and a person that possibly was raised by Lucifer sad, "Sign your name and sit down." And we sat unattended out in a waiting room for what seemed like an eternity.

Then, finally, our name is called and we follow the same person down a hallway to an 8-foot-by-8-foot cell, or maybe it's an examination room, where we sit down, the door was closed and we sat in this room for what seemed like another eternity as the walls closed in on us.

Then some person came in and took our blood pressure and drew blood and, once again, disappeared. By the way, I wonder what's happening to our blood pressure through the entire process. And then, finally, an uncaring doctor comes in, spends a couple of minutes with us and leaves. We're told to exit, pay the bill and that is the end of it.

What if the medical profession employed a Statement of Intent and told us what was going to take place while we visited? Would we not have felt better about the entire process? Would our blood pressure have not been more realistic or more normal when it was taken? Of course it would be. That's the reason for this technique.

It is no different than going into a store to buy a suit and a professional salesperson says, "Mr. or Mrs. Jones, what I would like to do is help you find a suit that is perfect for you. Then you'll try it on. After that, I'll lay out all the price and payment information so when you are ready to buy your new suit, you'll have everything you need to know. Fair enough?" "Fair enough"

No different than going to McDonald's and saying, "I want a milkshake. I'm interested in a milkshake." And the guy or young lady says, "What I'd like to do is help you find a milkshake that is prefect for you. What I'll do is I'll give you a taste of it and then I'll lay out all the price and payment information on your milkshake so when you are ready to get your milkshake, you'll have everything you need to know. Fair enough?" Fair enough.

The technique is bulletproof because the customer wants to bring up price. And, you have just told you are going to give them the price. They've heard how hard it is to get a price but you negated that by pro-actively telling them you would provide it. They want to look at cars and you told them you are going to help them look at cars. They want to drive one and you've told them they will. Most important, you have relieved all the pressure of them thinking you are going to 'trick' them into buying something they don't want because you told them you were going to give them all this information and then let them leave with it if they want to. The customer is going to think you are brand new and have no idea how to sell a car. This is a comfort area you have created for your customer and they will thank you for it.

Now after the Statement of Intent – and I want to do the statement once again, because I want to roll it into the second phase. Once again, "Mr. and Mrs. Customer, my name is, I've been at ABC Motors for 'X' number of years and I absolutely love what I do. What I would like to do is this: help you find a car that is just right for you and your family. I'll show it to you. We'll go over it. Then we'll drive it. When we're done with that, I'll lay out all the price and payment information so when you are ready to buy, you'll have all the facts. Fair enough?" Fair enough.

This technique is designed to put them at ease whereby when you're trying to establish value in your product, they will actually hear you and see the value instead of being distracted.

After you do your Statement of Intent, it rolls into another area that is vital to your success.

Let's take it a step further.

You ask, "Who is the vehicle for, sir? Is it for you or your wife?" You are trying to find the primary buyer – who is going to be driving the automobile. At this point, you might want to offer a cold drink or coffee and ask them to come inside so you can sit down and talk about what features, etc., are important to them. Why? Let them know, "This will help you and it will help me help you."

If you can get to this point, you have agreed on two important aspects. They have agreed to let me take them through a process that has no surprises and they've agreed to let me do some discovery so I can take them farther into the sale process itself.

The Statement of Intent is a very effective and disarming tool and it will provide comfort to the customer. It will also establish you as the servant, which is critical to your success.

CHAPTER ELEVEN

RECAP AND REVIEW

o   The Statement of Intent builds comfort.

o   I will use the Statement every time.

o   Customers want to know what's going to take place.

o   The Statement of Intent is the first agreement reached with the customer.

o   I've agreed to give them good service.

o   They agreed to let me take them through the process.

o   Fair enough? Fair enough.

CHAPTER 12

DISCOVERY

I like to call this the search for a genuine conversation regarding the client's actual needs. Customers can shop your car, they can shop the price of your car, but they can't shop your genuineness, your servant's heart or your care for their needs as shown by your true desire to help them.

Question quality is critical in the discovery process. I learned somewhere that the size of your pocketbook is directly proportional to the quality of questions you ask. It's never been more true than in the discovery step.

Selection of the automobile is very important, but there is a need to know who it is for and get a picture of what the customer truly wants. Is it a need? Is it a celebration? Or is it an emotional reward? Who's the vehicle for? Who will be the primary driver? What equipment is important to them? Do they like lighter or darker colors? And why are they getting a new car? What will they use it for? What are their wants and what are their needs?

Don't take lightly the questions of "Why are you getting a new car?" Few ask this question but it can open up lots of doors and provide insight, plus it gets the customer talking.

These are the most critical pieces of information to gain in the discovery process. For far too long in the automobile industry we were taught to ask low quality questions such as "What's your budget?" and "What price range are you looking for?" This method is totally wrong and will not work in today's environment.

For one thing, you have not earned the right to ask such questions. Besides, you could be backing yourself into a corner that you cannot come out of.

For instance, when Mr and Mrs. Jones made their blood oath about what they were and were not going to do they also discussed that they're paying $350 on their current vehicle and that they're willing to go to, say, $450. They also discussed that if the salesperson says anything about payment, Mr. Smith will say "We'd like the same payment." While Mrs. Smith will say, "We'd like it to be lower." If you ask price range, Mr. Smith will say "About $10,000," and Mrs. Smith will say, "Around $8,000" All of those prices are unrealistic and everyone knows it.

The short version of this lesson: Stay off price and find out what is important to them on their vehicle. Remember, price has to be set aside and put in its proper place. Establish value first, then present price.

A way to get genuine information on what their current position is to simply ask, "Are you currently making payments on your vehicle?" If so, "Do you mind if I ask what they are?" And whatever their payment is, you reply in a very sincere tone, "Wow! Those were the good old days." Leave it at that and never bring it up again.

Another quality question to ask is, "Will you possibly be trading in the car you drove in?" The answer to that question is usually "Yes." From there you ask the customer to show you their car.

I believe people are most comfortable talking about their own work, their home and family or their own automobile. Give them the chance to sell you their car. They will tell you things about themselves and their car that you could have never gotten out of them any other way. All of the good points and the bad points will come to the forefront.

During the show-and-tell of their car, price will come up again, so be ready. They can't help themselves. This is why we did a Statement of Intent. They are going to ask somewhere about the price of a certain car and you can respond, "As I promised you earlier, I'll lay out all of the pricing information. Fair enough?"

All during the Discovery Phase, we have to earn the right to ask certain questions. After we've earned the right, we can get more specific and more probing.

Really what we are trying to establish is a genuine conversation – that is what the Discovery Phase is all about. You want to know the customer's needs, wants and desires.

Try to get a sense of the real motive, whether it's truly a need or a celebration or and emotional reward they are trying to fill. That's why the helpfulness that we provide might just give them the opportunity to give us the answers to the puzzle.

When asking about what's important to them or what they need or what they want, guard against being too definitive. With the internet and all the information that is readily available to consumers, they come into dealerships with the idea in their mind that they're going to custom build an automobile. Therefore, our product knowledge with regard to different equipment packages is a critical part of handling today's modern customer. Because anything that the customer states they need or want, it's our job, our responsibility to broaden their statement to where we might fit one of our in-stock vehicles as a solution to this need or want.

As an example, let's say a customer comes in and tells you they are looking for a pink 1998 Ford Explorer. Well, heck, you don't have one of *those.* It might be a short visit if you are not on your toes. Your response should be something like, "Oh, you are looking for a small SUV that's pretty sporty or stands out? Is that correct?" You have to be able to broaden things a little bit.

Here is where having great product knowledge is so valuable. Customers will come in looking for a Sequoia with the XPD B14 package on it. That package might have a sunroof and air-conditioning as the critical components and it has minor components tied with it.

You have to be able to broaden the request so there may be a vehicle in stock you can show the customer. That is the reason that earlier the question "Is there a preference in lighter or darker colors?" was asked. If you simply ask "What color do you want?" then all of the sudden, you are limiting yourself.

Ask quality questions and get quality answers. And, attempt to make the conversation a genuine one.

CHAPTER TWELVE

RECAP AND REVIEW

o   Pursuit of a genuine conversation.

o   Quality questions are critical.

o   Don't "qualify." Investigate and discover.

o   I must earn the right to ask heavy questions.

o   The more the customer talks, the better I'm doing.

o   "Read" what they say.

o   Discover and assess their needs.

o   Uncover their motive.

o   I will be a generous listener.

CHAPTER 13

SELECTION

If you have completed the discovery process and needs assessment correctly, you should have a great picture of what the customer is looking for in an automobile: the type, what they'll be using it for and an understanding of what they are currently paying. Plus. We have an idea of their motive.

In the traditional setting, this is where we blow it, really lose the sale. Why? Because we wrongly make a decision about what they want and what they are not going to be able to afford. This is a horrible assumption on our part. We are not even close to the actual buying part. We are still earning confidence and gaining trust from the customer.

I would rather have a customer excited about the wrong car than having told them about the 'right' car and then watch them drive off the lot because I told them something they did not want to hear. You are better off having someone excited and still sitting there with you – even if it is the wrong car. People spend crazy amounts of money when they're excited.

During the selection process, you are looking for "yes momentum." Remember that the customer's idea is always better than yours. If they are looking for a used vehicle, take them to it and let them know the price. Use your greatest skills to show the value they are getting for their money. Hopefully, they'll want to go even further on the vehicle.

If they are looking at new cars, use your same techniques. Keep in mind to continue to clarify as they select vehicles. As the decision is narrowed and maybe the car seems too expensive for the customer, here is a technique that can help you move to another vehicle that may be more in their budget without insulting them.

For example, the customers are looking at a Chevy Impala and you feel it might be a little bit too much for them. "Before I show you the Impala, and we pick out an Impala, would you prefer to see the Malibu? It will save you a couple thousand dollars and $30-40 per month. Would you like to see the Malibu?" This technique will allow them to move themselves. Maybe they will like the Malibu. They will probably move down in car. But, if they don't and you sense that the Impala is too much for them, remind them they can always go back to the Malibu.

If you happen to be unsuccessful in getting them to move themselves, try saying "Let's think this over a minute (and, believe me, later on when you don't want to hear it, they're going to tell you they want to think it over). If you think the Impala is the car that is going to be right for you, you might need to be a little flexible on your payment planning."

Here is what is happening right now and it is critical: Keep clarifying. Keep offering switch ideas until you're in a vehicle that excites them. But, at the worst case, whatever they are looking at, make sure they are excited.

One area of adding energy at this time in the selection process is something pretty corny but it's a tried and true means of adding energy into the process.

"You know, Mr. and Mrs. Jones, I've certainly enjoyed working with you today. I hope you are having a good time. But, in working with you, I kind of sense a celebration. Is it a birthday? Or maybe an anniversary? What is it?"

That often will uncover some drive or motive that we can further energize the car transaction right here. They're going to continue with price questions, and be prepared to set the price questions aside. Remember, their price questions are only reflex objections on their part.

Another way to handle this situation is to simply say," Mr. and Mrs. Jones, I appreciate that price is very important to you. As I mentioned before, I'm going to get you the best price on yours and on ours and estimates on the rates and payments. Would that be all right with you? Fair enough?" Fair enough.

Hopefully, at this point, prior to presenting the vehicle, we have the price issue set aside.

We still need value first – then price.

CHAPTER THIRTEEN

RECAP AND REVIEW

o   We have the picture of what they want, let's help them find it.

o   We gain trust by proving that we've listened.

o   Think about what I know, talk about what sells.

o   I must put them on a car that excites them.

o   I am looking for "Yes" momentum.

o   I must set price aside.

o   Excitement.

CHAPTER 14

PRESENTATION

Simply put, this is where many of the sales are won or lost. Generally speaking, this step will determine what price we sell the car for.

In presenting the vehicle, you are setting every thing into motion – all that you have worked for and what you are going to do next. You have to make the price of the product appear to be a bargain versus the value the customer perceives in the car. You have to present the car in a manner where you always remember what is important to that specific customer. If you've done your work to this point, the presentation will be like a slam dunk in the NBA – very few misses.

Here is a statistical note to keep in mind: of the car buying public, 80 percent say they got a lousy presentation of their vehicle they purchased. Talk about an opportunity to be outstanding! I am talking about a time to have the full attention of the customer; it can't get any better than this! You are going to make sure they see the value!

Having said that, keep in mind that today's customer comes fairly well armed with product information. That is why your product knowledge is critical. This is your opportunity to shine. This is where you can stand out from the crowd. This is where you make your money.

Remember what is <u>important to them</u> and go sell a car!

Here is the basic method of presentation.

If you're looking at a pre-owned vehicle, the basic approach is to start with the price marked on the vehicle and share with the customer the value they are getting. It is important to remember that people who are buying a used car are really buying a new car in their view. There has to be the same excitement level on the $3,000 car as there is in the $30,000. From my view, if you are selling a $20,000 car, make a $30,000 presentation; if you are selling a $30,000 car, make a $40,000 presentation. You get the idea.

I had a great salesman tell me the difference between a $10 haircut and a $40 haircut. With the $10 haircut, the guy pulled out some electric clippers, buzzed around your head and was done in minutes. With the $40 haircut, the person will get down on one knee and look at you from different angles, feel this and pull that, tug at your collar and then pull out the clippers and be done in minutes. YOU get four times the value, though. Give 'em a $40 haircut, not a $10 one.

If the customer is looking for a new vehicle, it's best to start with the price displayed on the vehicle again. If it lists for $25,000, explain that it was designed to sell for $28,000 but it only priced at $25,000. Show them what they are going to get for their money. The price issue is going to come up again so you might as well lead them to it. They are going to ask about getting the best price. They can't help themselves.

Dustins $7 cut + 20$ tip (for missing chunks of hair) was not a great value

78

"OK, now I won't hold you to it, of course," they will say. "But can you just give me a ballpark what you can do with regard to price?

You have to address it and set it aside. "As I promised you, Mr. and Mrs. Smith, I'm going to lay out all of the pricing information for you. I'm going to give you the best price on ours and the best price on yours, plus the payments and rates. We have a very strict policy here at ABC Motors not to mislead our customers. I promise to you I'll lay it all out for you and give you copies if you'd like. Fair enough?" Fair enough. The price issue must be set aside or they <u>will</u> <u>not</u> hear the value you're selling.

When you are showing the automobile, you have to talk about value, value and value. Don't talk money, talk value. People do not buy features. <u>They buy what the feature does for them.</u> Paint the picture for them then tie the feature and its benefit down with a confirming question: "Mr. Customer, can you see some value to...?" This is a must.

It is also important in the presentation that, along with value and proper walk around, that you cover each and every area that is important to the customers. Be clear when you do this. "Mr. and Mrs. Smith, you told me you wanted a sunroof. This one fully retracts, is tinted and has a flip up feature that allows you to create an airflow without fully opening the sunroof." Whatever it is, make sure <u>they</u> <u>know</u> that <u>you</u> <u>know</u> it is something they want.

This will differentiate you from the competition because you are listening and giving them service like they have never before experienced.

You also need to cut out the competition by telling them confirming features of your car that differentiates you. "This is the only car in its class that has a one-inch screw in this location." or whatever. Maybe it is the only car that has a one-inch button on the radio. You have to cut out the competition.

Another area of importance during the presentation is to build more trust and strut your stuff with regard to product knowledge. The best way to do that is, for each vehicle, choose one immediately verifiable fact that you can show the customer in an instant that is real and unique.

A good example of this is in trucks. All truck have axle weight ratings on a sticker in the doorjamb. You can sound and appear as though you are the most truck-smart person on the planet if you know those ratings for each truck. Because, once you tell them, you go to the sticker and point it out to them. Boom! Instant credibility!

This gives the customer a comfort level with you that cannot be replaced. First you mention it and now you prove it. That is how the wall of credibility is built – brick by brick. During all great performances there is a tipping point where the customer becomes completely involved. These are often brought on by immediately verifiable product information.

CHAPTER FOURTEEN

RECAP AND REVIEW

o Value, value, value.

o Nail what's important to them.

o I must give a dynamic presentation.

o Give a $40 haircut.

o I must set price aside.

o I must stay off price and establish value

o Keep clarifying you are on the right car.

o Product feature and what it does for them.

o Look for the tipping point.

CHAPTER 15

DEMONSTRATION

There is one major reason the demonstration is so important. Hopefully, we're on a specific vehicle and the demonstration is where we bring it all home.

Let me share with you a statistical reason and verification of the value and importance of the demo drive.

In 1998, there was a study where the Honda Accord and Toyota Camry were being compared by 700 customers. Pictures and information about the vehicles we're provided, both on the Accord and Camry, along with the pricing information. Without driving either vehicle and using only the pictures, information and prices, 53 percent of the people selected the Accord.

Now the survey group was given the chance to drive both vehicles. After doing so, and still using the pictures, information and pricing along with <u>having driven</u> both cars, 90 percent of the group selected the Camry. What does that survey prove? The proof is in the driving.

That is the major reason you have to be connected to your customer at this point in the selling process. If you have <u>built</u> <u>rapport</u> and trust, they <u>will</u> allow you to finish the sales process.

Prior to driving the car it is imperative that you offer the customer an opportunity to switch vehicles one more time. like!

Let's go back to the Impala vs. Malibu example.

"Mr. and Mrs. Smith, before we drive your Impala, would you like to look at the Malibu? It could save you a couple thousand dollars and maybe $30 or $40 a month. Would you like to see the Malibu?" At which time they will tell you, yes and <u>you'll</u> <u>know</u> price is very important to them, or no, they want the Impala. Psychological terrorism ☺

This process of offering alternative saving vehicles is going to be critical in the closing stages. When we get down to closing the deal on the Impala, the customer will not or should not be asking about saving money because <u>I have already offered to save them money.</u> <u>They told me they wanted to pay for the Impala.</u>

Demonstration drives are just that, demonstration drives. They are meant for the salesperson to drive first and demonstrate the various features of the vehicle. Because you listened earlier, you already know they are going to take it on trips to the mountains and back and forth to school or that gas mileage is very important. By listening, the demonstration drive should really take care of itself. Don't ask to demonstrate a vehicle, assume it. You've already discussed it and they're going to buy this car.

Here is how I do it.

If the customer tells you they have driven their neighbor's car that is just like this one, remind them of the Intent Statement. You already talked about driving one and now let's have some fun. Because, remember, if they don't drive it, they're not going to buy it.

Start out by driving and demonstrating the different items they told you were important. At some point, stop the vehicle and put the primary driver in the driver's seat (in this example it's Mrs. Smith). Adjust all of the seats and seatbelts. Program in her favorite radio station and show her how it is done. Go over all of the convenience features in the car, the entire time she is in the driver's seat, with her favorite radio station playing the background.

Very well researched tactic, all major department stores use it!

Then you get in the back seat because you are about to watch the best movie you've ever seen. You are going to see the customers put themselves in the picture. Body language is very important at this point. Watch both him and her. Make sure they are comfortable and not fidgeting around.

It is very important to go on the demonstration drive because you need to know if there is any objection to the vehicle.

"Are there any questions you have, Mr. and Mrs. Smith?" you ask as you ride along. Your conversation <u>needs</u> to be very limited. The customer is in control right now, both figuratively and literally.

On the way back to the dealership, you quickly ask <u>if they liked</u> <u>the vehicle</u> and then watch the body language. I'm reading them. Then you quickly and abruptly ask, "Do you want to own it?" with no follow-up. You want to hear their answer and see their body language. If they look at each other, things are going your way. *Interesting!,*

In reality, the demonstration drive is one of the most simple yet most crucial parts of the selling process. Make sure the customer understands the convenience features and how all of the simple controls work. Confirm with them that they see value in each and every one of those features. Put them in the picture and allow them to see themselves in that picture.

Also remember cupholders are extremely important to women for some reason so always point them out ☺

I first fell in love with Saab over a cupholder ☺

CHAPTER FIFTEEN

RECAP AND REVIEW

o   If they don't drive, they won't buy.

o   The demo drive brings it home.

o   The demo puts them in the picture.

o   Switch again early.

o   The demo drive confirms the value and justifies the price.

o   Listen and observe on the demo drive.

o   Allow them to take mental ownership.

CHAPTER 16

TRIAL CLOSE

Trial closes are some of those questions that need to be asked, even though salespeople are often afraid to ask them. The true beauty of the trial close is rather than the old-fashioned "So, do you wanna buy this car?" approach, the trial close is only asking for an opinion, which is far less threatening than asking people to sign their life away.

"Is there anything , Mr. and Mrs. Jones, that you like least about the vehicle?" Make sure you ask this question and then listen. Whatever it is, if you feel it is minor, ask the simple question: "Would it keep you from owning it? What's your opinion Mrs. Jones?"

After driving the vehicle and looking at the car, trial closes are as simple as, "Mrs. Jones, what did you like best about the vehicle?" Ask Mr. Jones the same question. These are non-threatening, yet telling questions. Ask each person their opinion or feelings. Then questions get more to the point. "Is this a car you think you would like to own? Is this something you would like to have in your driveway?"

Then ask the genuine question: "Mr. and Mrs. Jones, provided the payments meet your expectation, is this the car you would like to have today? If I understand you correctly, and please tell me if I'm wrong, I understand this is the car you would like to buy, provided the price is right. Is that correct?"

Another way to get to it is: "Is there anything, Mr. and Mrs. Jones, other than price and payment, that would keep you from owning this vehicle right now?"

These are very important questions to ask and it must be done in a timely fashion, right after the demonstration drive.

The questions we just talked about are questions most salespeople do not have the courage ask. But, it is critical to ask them because there needs to be time for clarification. If there is not clarification, you could be in the write up stage, present figures that are acceptable and all of the sudden, Mrs. Jones says, "Yes, but I wanted yellow."

Here are a few other minor trial closing techniques.

When a customer has a minor objection such as the car is not the favorite color or they don't want a sunroof, here is how you can handle those situation.

"I can appreciate what you say, Mr. and Mrs. Jones, and I understand, but may I ask you a genuine question. Would you own this one?"

Often in the automobile business, a salesperson would say something like, "If I could make the price and everything right on this one, would you own it?" Or my personal favorite (Ha! Ha!): "Could you be a little color-blind if I could save you some money?"

Both of those questions bastardize your own product and uses your idea instead of the customer's. I recommended my technique whereby we end up in the same place, but I want the customer to <u>instigate</u> the saving money. Make it their idea!

Let's go back. The color is wrong and after you ask the customer if they would own it anyway, 90 percent of them are going to say, "Well, yeah, but the price better be right" or "You're going to have to give me a good deal."

Whose idea is always better? The customer's. You want them that much further into the buying process. You want them to take mental ownership because in every automobile transactions, there is a very definitive line. The customer buys the vehicle mentally <u>and then, and only then,</u> do you fine-tune the dollars and cents.

Anything prior to that point cheapens the product and lessens their value perception.

So let's go back to the sunroof. "Would you own it? Could you see yourself driving this one?" You need to stress the resale value of the sunroof and the enjoyment. "Mr. and Mrs. Wilson, would you own this car?"

If everything else is right and we're only dealing with a minor objection, I promise you they will say something like, "Well, you better not charge me for it" or "You better make the price right." All you want is the client's commitment.

Immediately upon their response, if the dollars are right or the payment is in line with them, you say, "Well, come on folks, let me show you how easy it is to own it." It must be done this way.

CHAPTER SIXTEEN

RECAP AND REVIEW

o   Maintain "yes" momentum.

o   I must clarify with trial closes.

o   Opinions and feelings uncover motives.

o   I must trial close to know whether or not we're on the right car.

o   Would they own "this" car?

o   Must reduce to dollars.

o   It must be their idea.

CHAPTER 17

WRITE-UP

The Write-up is a very time sensitive step in the sale process. Ideally, you will spend about 90 percent of your time building rapport, discovering the customer's needs and wants, helping select a vehicle, presenting the vehicle, demonstrating the vehicle – in other words, selling the vehicle. The other 10 percent will be spent writing it up, fine tuning the price and delivering them the car. It's very time sensitive.

It's also a critical step in that people have been sold a car without good rapport. They have also been sold a car without a good presentation or a demonstration drive. But, there has never, ever – and I mean never, ever – been a car sold without giving someone a price.

It is important to have the information from their trade-in. We made note while they were selling it and we have the Vehicle Identification Number (VIN) and the miles. All of this is important.

You have to put everyone on paper and write them up. Some folks don't want to get put on paper and don't want to be written up. Some folks just want the heck out of there because they know they cannot say no.

There is also a portion of the public who consider themselves the greatest negotiators in the free world.

I want to put <u>everyone on paper</u>. And, everyone can be written up by the use of a couple of simple techniques. How do I put them on paper and get them to the write-up?

Often times after a demonstration drive, a customer says, "Thank you very much. You're the best salesperson I've ever had and we want to go think about it."

"Well, Mr. and Mrs. Jones, let me give you the price and payment information like I promised you I would."

"Oh, that's not necessary," they'll say.

"Mr. and Mrs. Jones, we've spent this time together and it only takes a moment. I want to give you the price and payments so you have it to think over while you are at home." A statement like that makes them feel much more comfortable.

Another customer may not want to get into payments.

"Well, Mr. and Mrs. Jones, let me tell you how simple this whole thing is. I'm going to lay it out for you and you know how to say 'No' don't you? So if it doesn't make sense to you would you just tell me 'No.' Could you tell me 'No?' And if it does make sense, maybe it is something you want to do, but let me provide that information for you. Fair enough?" Fair enough.

One of the things I have learned in my 30-some years in the automobile industry is that the cash from a customer is my favorite thing. It is very important, too. The clients have already had discussions of how much money they are going to put down. And when they made their pact prior to coming to the dealership they agreed on something.

"If we get a salesperson who asks us where we want to be on our payments, I'll say 'The same,' and you tell them 'Less.'"

If I ask a customer how much money they want to put down (which I consider a low quality question), what do you think the customer's response will be? I'll guarantee you the answer will be , "Nothing." No one wants to spend money so they don't want to put any money down. Now, they've already discussed it and they have agreed they are going to put $3,000 down but when I ask them they will tell me "Nothing."

As I am writing up the paperwork, I'm going to say, looking them dead in the eye: "You know, Mr. and Mrs. Jones, on a transaction like this, most of my clients will put between $6,000 and $7,000 down and some as little as three or four thousand. Where do you see yourself?" One of them will spill it. If one of them doesn't, your follow-up question should be: "Should the lending institution ask us for four or five thousand dollars down, how should we respond?"

I promise you, you will know how much down payment there is after those two questions

Cash is your friend, for a lot of reasons. It lowers the payment. It helps everyone.

CHAPTER SEVENTEEN

RECAP AND REVIEW

o   I must put them all on paper.

o   Ninety percent of time is spent on the lot, ten percent with the write-up.

o   Must be timely.

o   I know right now if I have a deal.

o   Ask for cash.

o   Casual confidence.

o   Be neat and professional.

CHAPTER 18

PRESENTATION OF FIGURES AND ASKING FOR THE BUSINESS

The great part about this step of the sale process is you already know in your heart whether or not you have a car deal. You know if you've missed any steps and you know if you have them in the right car. And, you know if they have mental ownership.

Please hear this: From this point forward, you will get the outcome you expect. Presentation of figures must be done in a timely manner, with the casual confidence in your presentation and expectant eyes looking for the "yes."

Prior to going to get the figures, it's important to have a conversation with your clients, such as this:

"I'm going to go get you your payment figures, along with the price. We'll go over them when I get back and you can tell me which terms are best for you and which ones you want to go with. Fair enough?" Fair enough.

The assumption is critical at this point. Customers can smell rats.

Upon leaving your clients, you hand them your evidence manual and give them some opportunities to see what you are as a person, as evidence of what you've tried to establish earlier by your words and actions. Make them feel a sense of transparency in all you do, particularly at the price presentation.

This may sound absurd, but it is true: Statistics show more than 50 percent of the time, a horrible mistake is made by salespeople in this step of the process. They present the price and payments, but, if you can imagine, they don't ask the customer to buy. They forget or neglect to ask them.

How to ask for the business

1. Which payment do you want to go with?

2. Why don't you start enjoying right now?

3. I'll get us a cold drink while we finish up your paperwork, fair enough? Congratulations!

4. Have I earned your business? Congratulations.

5. I'll send for your new car to be cleaned up while we finish your paperwork. Fair enough?

6. From everything you've told me, we found the perfect car. Let's go ahead and finish up your paperwork.

7. You deserve this. You're doing the right thing.

8. I need your OK right here.

9. Let me have a copy of your driver's license and insurance card so we can finish up you paperwork.

10. What time of the month do you want your first payment to start? Great. Congratulations.

The way to ask is show the payment choices, show them the price and if it's payments, "Which one is best for you? Which one do you want to go with?" But most certainly, ask them to buy. "You deserve it. Why don't you start enjoying your new car?"

Sometimes the customer will say 'no.' "You know, we just need to think about it," when, in fact, they are saying, "Hold on a minute. Wait a minute." They still have little areas of fear.

Remember, they have a fear of making the wrong choice or making a mistake, so this "we need to think about it," is really a "Hold on a moment." Now that we've asked them once, in most cases, we need to be prepared to gently ask them five, six or seven times.

The average car sale is closed after the fifth 'no.' You wouldn't think that. I am such a buyer when I go out; I just buy stuff and get on with it. But, people want to be reassured that they are doing the right thing. Don't rush it. Present the figures and ask them to buy.

Both the customer and you will be happy that you asked them one more time.

CHAPTER EIGHTEEN

RECAP AND REVIEW

o   I already know I've got a deal. Bring it home!

o   Casual confidence.

o   Matter of fact, make a choice.

o   Maintain transparency.

o   Ask them to buy.

o   Reinforce they're doing the right thing.

o   My rapport/value report cards.

CHAPTER 19

THE CLOSING

Closing the deal is taking all of the rough edges off and confirming to them and with them that they are doing the right thing. Believe me, every customer was taught to say, whether it's by clergy or the guy at the dry cleaners, the price is too high, the trade is too low and the payment is way off. In reality, they don't know what else to say.

There is a sequence that must be used in any and all of these situations. For instance, let's start with 'The price is too high.'

You say, "Remember the Impala and the Malibu? Let's go look at that Malibu I was telling you about. That is going to save you a couple thousand dollars right there." Whereby, they're going to say, "We don't want the Malibu, we want the Impala."

"Well, Mr. and Mrs. Jones, you're going to have to pay for the Impala." (Say it politely.)

Get the drift? We're giving them what they want. They have seen the value. If they want to save money, we offered them a way. But, let's go back to the real world.

We tried to put them back to the Malibu and they said they wanted the Impala. Respond with value. Now, I am going to verbally sell this Impala again and what they're getting for their money.

I respond with a third party story to substantiate the value I've already sold.

"I've had people try to cut corners before, when, in fact, they were not happy in the end. Mr. and Mrs. Jones, the Impala has everything you're looking for. Why don't I get you a cold Coke while we finish up you paper work? Fair enough?" Fair enough.

They don't buy that. "The trade is too low."

"I understand. Everyone has hopeful expectations for their trades." Again, I substantiate it with a third party story. "I had a client in here not too long ago that had a vehicle similar to yours. We were unable to give them anywhere near this kind of money." Then ask them to buy again.

The objection sequence, whether it's price, trade or payment, is always done in this manner. Go back to value, a third party story to substantiate the value and them ask them to buy, again. This represents tremendous value to the customer and, it's something we can live with. Ask again.

There's an area with regard to trade-in that's sometimes handy for the people who say, "Well, I could sell my car for 'X' amount of dollars." It is a method called ATRAPT.

Here is the way it works. Stay with me because it makes sense in the end. Follow along by writing the numbers on a separate piece of paper.

We have a customer that we are giving $9000 for his car and he thinks he could sell it for $11,000, if not more.

"Sir, that make sense because $2,000 is $2,000. I'm doing the very best by you that I can. And, if you could sell your car for $11,500, that $2,500 difference makes some sense.

"But let me ask you a question. If you put that car in your driveway with a 'For Sale' sign, what would you ask for it?

That's what the 'A' in ATRAPT stand for. What would you ask for it?

He would say, "Eleven-five."

"That's great, sir. That's $2,500 to the good. Heck, fire, you're better off that way.

"But, let me ask you another question. Say a guy came onto you driveway with cash and said, "I'm ready to buy your car. What would you take for it?"

And that is what the 'T' in ATRAPT stands for: What would you take for it?

"Would you take ten-five?" the guy asks.

"No I wouldn't take ten-five. Might take eleven," says your customer.

Then you say, "I mean, really, sir, the guy said he would give you $10,800 and you would say no? To cash?"

"Well," your customer would say, "I might take it."

"If you did," you say, "that's still $1,800 better off and you're a heck of a lot better off that me giving you nine."

"Darn right it is," he says.

Then you continue to set the scene.

"Let me ask you, if we went and looked at your car and it needed new tires. What if the guy said, 'I'll give you ten-eight, but I need new tires."

The 'R' in ATRAPT stands for reconditioning.

"Would you give him new tires or would you hold firm?"

"I would hold firm," he would say.

"If he asked you for $400 worth of tires?"

"Well, I could get them for less than that."

"OK," you would say, "let's say maybe after these tires you are getting ten-six, you're still $1,600 better off that you were, right?

"Let me ask you this, where would you advertise that your car is for sale?"

That is the 'A' in ATRAPT.

Would you put it in the paper?"

"Yes, I would put it in the paper."

"If you put it in the paper – we put ads in the paper and they cost $50 for a weekend for a car ad. Now, on average, it takes us 90 days to sell our cars. How long do you think it would take you to sell yours?"

"I would sell it in a month."

"If you do sell it in a month, that is four time $50. You'd spend $200 on advertising. But that makes sense because you would still get your ten-six. Wouldn't you?"

"Darn right," he would say.

"So now you are getting ten-four and you are still $1,400 better off."

"Yes, I am," he says.

"Are you currently making payments, sir?"

"Well, yeah."

That's what the P in ATRAPT stands for – payment.

"What is your payment?"

"Three hundred dollars."

"Well, you're going to be making another payment between now and then and we were going to pay it off today. So now, instead of ten-four, you're actually getting ten-one because you're making another payment. But, you are still better off, though. You are still $1,100 better off.

"But you know what, sir, if you traded it today, you only have to pay tax on the difference because you have a tax advantage for trading the car." That is what the final 'T' stands for in ATRAPT.

" And, that tax advantage would be $650 because you're not paying tax on your trade. So you will only get $9,500 for your car by selling it yourself.

"What are we fussing about? Five hundred dollars?"

You can move anyone with this method on a used car.

Customers all have a different means of being closed. Remember from when we talked earlier, everybody who gets sold take delivery. Closing is one of the little steps that we fine-tune the figures and take the edge off the transaction.

Customers need to be reminded that they need to be flexible with themselves. "Goodness gracious, this is the car you've always wanted. Why are you selling yourself short for just this little bit?"

If you sense you're a long way from a 'yes.' turn the money page over and talk about something else. You can always come back and reignite the car because you don't want to beat up the figures. You might want to take them to the car again to reignite them <u>The car is your friend.</u> "Come with me. I forgot to show you something on your car," you could say to them.

Another means of clarification and putting the customer on the spot in a very gentle manner is to ask them if you helped them select the wrong car.

"Mr. and Mrs. Jones, did I help you pick out the wrong car?" Their reply is either going to be a 'yes' or a 'no.' Either way, you need to know.

Usually, customers are just concerned – concerned about making a wrong decision and making a mistake.

Another objection is the customer will tell you they need to go shop two other dealerships to compare prices or whatever.

Your response is very simple. "Well, Mr. and Mrs. Jones, let me tell you this is a very competitive industry and I can't give you a price that you can't beat."

"What do you mean? Is that your rock bottom price?"

Then you just pull the rug out from under them by saying, "Folks, I can't give you a price you can't beat, nor can anyone else."

Let me tell you how simple this is. The automobile industry is very competitive. You simply state: "I can give you what I've given you. It is a very fair price. It represents tremendous value to you and it's something we can live with. But, you can jump in your car, drive and hour or so and do this all over again so someone can save you two or three or four hundred dollars. And, two or three, four hundred dollars is two or three, four hundred dollars.

"But you know what? You don't have to stop there. You can jump in your car and drive another hour or so and spend another two or three hours doing this and you might save another hundred dollars more. But don't stop there. Get in your car and drive another hour or so and someone will save you 50 or 75 dollars. But don't stop there.

"Now, what in the world are you doing? What are we talking about? Let me ask you: What if I saved you about 10 hours of driving and about 20 hours of aggravation and maybe, just maybe, I could save you a couple hundred dollars right here," is another way to approach it.

Then you'll get what's called the flat line objection. It's kind of like that monitor in the hospital on the televison shows that has a steady beeeeeeeeep, a flat green line and no heartbeat.

The customer will tell you that you are the best salesperson they have ever had and that they "want to think about it." Or they've "never bought a car on the first day." Or "our family always discusses these type of purchases." They will tell you everything but you are not the best salesperson because you did not get them to say 'Yes.'

How do you deal with the flat line? Here is what I do.

"You know, Mr. and Mrs. Jones, when you started your journey to find that right car at an affordable price. Based on what you've told me, you've accomplished it. Instead of fretting about it and sweating it out, why don't you go ahead and start enjoying it. Fair enough?"

"No."

"I appreciate what you say and I understand. But you know, Mr. and Mrs. Jones, I'm a consumer just like you and often times I've found myself telling a salesperson that I wanted to think about it, I needed to sleep on it or whatever. I did that just to be polite, like you are being to me. When, in fact, it was either the product I was looking at or it was the money. Now, which is it?"

Flat lines are the toughest. The only reason they're saying they've got to think about it, they've got to sleep on it is they're not saying 'no.' They're saying 'not yet."

A good technique to be used with some flat lines is to go ahead and give them a little rope. Have you ever been deep sea fishing and the fish was a little bit too big and too lively to be put in the boat? You need to give them some line so you can land them.

I'm going to start the process of walking them out to their car and making them feel that it is all over. Before I get too far, I'm going to stop and ask a simple question.

"Mr. and Mrs. Jones, I can't believe it but I forgot to ask you if you had any ideas as to how we could have put this deal together?"

I'm telling you right now it is money. They are too polite and too real. They don't want to come off too abrasively about asking for some money.

Give them a chance for an idea, because if this doesn't grab them, one more time on the way to their car, I'm going to ask them about the perfect world.

"Mr. and Mrs. Jones, I know there is no such thing as a perfect world, but if there was, how could we have put this together?"

They will come up with something.

Remember what we have learned: The customer's idea is better than ours. I need it to come out of their mouth. Anything I do price-wise is only cheapening the product. You cannot afford to do this in either the long- or short-term.

Now the customer gives me some terms other than what I presented and we can start doing business. After you hear their suggestion, you need to lighten the mood and create some flexibility. But, they have bought into buying. Now they are a buyer. They have shown to God, themselves, one another and to me that they are ready to dance. Instead of just sticking their toe into the swimming pool, they have shown me now they're ready to jump in and swim.

But now I'm going to try and take away access to the swimming pool by saying something like, "Well, of course you would." And then I'm going to come back and tighten it up.

"So if I understand you correctly, Mr. and Mrs. Jones, and correct me if I am wrong, at this price or at this payment, you're telling me I could earn your business <u>right now</u>, is that correct?"

"Yes, that's right."

"Well, I don't know that I can. I can possibly get close to it."

They'll say something like, "Oh no, you have to...."

Whatever their comment is, I'm going to restate it again. "So then, if I understand you, at this price, this payment, I can earn your business <u>right now</u>, correct?"

"Correct."

"Let me write a little note to my boss just so he'll understand what we're doing." This is called a note of commitment. "Mr. and Mrs. Jones will take delivery <u>right</u> <u>now</u>," with a great big toothy "<u>right</u> <u>now</u>, at such and such a price, payment and term. Is that correct?"

"Yes, it is."

"Let me have your OK right here." Get them to sign something.

In that one step, they have mentally purchased. They have told me they want to get into the swimming pool. And, I want to know they are getting in.

The note of commitment becomes critical. In the old days of the car business, they would call it 'the glue.' Get a check or a credit card or something that will make the deal 'stick together.'

I honestly think today's buyer is a little more sophisticated than that and I don't think they'll stand for it. I don't think they respect it, either. But, they do respect the fact that you ask them for their business.

CHAPTER NINETEEN

RECAP AND REVIEW

o   They are doing the right thing.

o   Objection sequence.

o   5 times is what it takes.

o   If they're sitting there, they want to own it.

o   The car is your friend.

o   Allow them time to get comfortable with their decision to buy.

o   Let them bring up money, you talk value.

o   When they nibble: restate, clarify and close.

o   I must get a note of commitment.

CHAPTER 20

DELIVERY

Please, please, please make the delivery of your customer's car the highlight of the entire experience. This is what they came for. They are paying dearly for their dream. They did us a favor; we didn't do them a favor.

One thing is true with regard to people and buying cars. Every customer that ever bought a car has the feeling that once they have my money, the salesperson and dealership does not care about them anymore. Your livelihood, your longevity in the car business and your ultimate success is based on how great an experience it was for your client.

Take your time at delivery because they expect otherwise. Show them how all the little controls work and let them know they're not going to remember everything you show them today. Tell them it is OK to call you with questions. Tell them that their delight with this new automobile is of the utmost importance to you.

One thing is for sure in the car business – you can replace any car you have, but you can never replace a customer or the value they represent to you.

CHAPTER TWENTY

RECAP AND REVIEW

o   Make it an event.

o   The customer did you a favor.

o   Great active delivery.

o   I will give them all the attention they need.

o   There is no dollar value that can be assigned to the value of a customer.

o   They're in your family of customers now.

CHAPTER 21

UNSOLD WRITE-UPS & FOLLOW-UP

This is an enormous pool of opportunity. For whatever reason, we didn't or were not able to completely engage the customer in the sales process. Hopefully, you were able to get a name, telephone number, etc., as a means to follow-up with them.

Why was I unable to engage them?

How was my attitude?

Was I engaged and focused?

Did I fall for a reflex, one-line close and fail to give my best?

It is critical to understand that it is our responsibility to adapt to the prospect no matter what they bring to the table. Some of them are "barkers" who are rude and rough to us which could catch us off guard. With that type of attitude, we could get caught off guard, whereby we give up and the opportunity just melts away right at the point of contact.

"Barkers" can sometimes be handled by apologizing for how they might have been treated at other dealerships, explaining to them that you don't take hostages and, finally, with strong eye contact asking them how they would like to be treated. From there, you confirm with them that that's the way you'll do it.

Others are "pukers" who provide a never ending series of reflex objections and sweep you away with statements like, "We just don't' know what we want," or "Not today," or We have to talk to Aunt Sadie," whereby you just give up. Statistic: 86 percent of customers buy something other than what the initially stated.

The last group is the so-called product specific prospect who discouraged us with their seemingly specific request. We got caught off guard and gave up.

All of these people <u>are</u> buyers. We missed the first time but we must follow-up in a hurry. We might have set up the next salesperson!

<u>The answer is rapport!</u> If you had focused first on making a friend and building rapport, you wouldn't be in this situation. <u>You would have sold them a vehicle using the process!</u>

<u>The number one reason prospects cut us short of completing the process is simple:</u>

<u>NO RAPPORT AND NOT IMPRESSED WITH YOU.</u>
<u>PERIOD.</u>

UN-SOLD WRITE-UP

These are the best prospects you'll ever have. They are close to buying. Follow-up fast and furiously with simple questions like:

When do you want to come in and get the car?

When do you want to get together again?

I have some new information for you.

FOLLOW-UP

The great thing about follow-up is that when you do it, you are among the first to do it, or you are in an extremely small group.

Simple, fool-proof follow-up

1. Tail light phone call – Immediately upon the customer leaving, call their home and leave some sort of message of their recorder. Ask them to call you. Tell them you enjoyed working with them. That you are looking forward to getting together with them soon. Something to show you are still interested.

2. Hand written note – Immediately after leaving the tail-light call, mail them an extremely short hand written note. Make it sincere and short.

3. Next day call – Yes, next day! You will never be bothering a prospect; you only "bother" someone who doesn't want to buy from you.

The key to follow-up is discipline on your part. You must diligently, religiously, consistently do what was just laid out for you.

CHAPTER TWENTY ONE

RECAP AND REVIEW

o   Unsold write-up's are my best prospects.

o   When I call, I'm the first one to follow up.

o   Tail light.

o   Hand written notes.

o   You'll never bother a real potential buyer.

CHAPTER 22

IF YOU ARE IN A SLUMP

The entire world runs in seasons. That is, most everything is cyclical. The same is true for selling cars.

First of all, be accountable. It's always us, it's never them. This is the mind set that's critical for growth and long lasting success.

A great philosopher, Yogi Berra, said it best:"I ain't in no slump, I just ain't hittin'" He also had another saying that is a foundation to success and that is," Where ever you are, be there." That means to be present and engaged.

Let's examine this condition called a sale slump.

Deals are going down all around you. The public is the same. The product is the same. You've got the same prospects, products and managers as everyone else. But, you're not selling and feel as though you better get out of the business because you think you'll never sell another car. You are hoping for a "lay down" just to get through the day. WOW!

WOW! is right. We better start at the source and get this thing fixed!

We know what our mind set is – it's awful. Remember CAFÉ and here is an additional approach to a cure.

1. Ask yourself what kind of day it is? Horrible, good, bad, great – whatever. Ask yourself how business is. You'd better say "Great!" because the last you had was great and wonderful.

Now what is you dominate thought? Better find the correct one. Count your blessings and be thankful. Be thrilled to be a part of the day.

2. Are you being a servant? You must approach and interact with prospects with a servant's heart. They can sense your motive.

3. Are you being a generous listener? You have to recognize that you listen people into rapport. You listen them into telling you how to sell them. Also, you listen them into all the steps of the process. Which brings me to this point:

4. How are your fundamentals (not pre-judging, product knowledge, skills, etc.)? Have you lost the edge? And secondly, are you skipping steps? There is only one short cut to a sale. This is to take no short cuts.

5. Finally, how do you feel about yourself? Are you good to yourself, your family, your friends and associates? Do you try to always do the right thing? Believe me, there is no particular season for doing the right thing. This must define you. If so, you'll feel good about yourself first. You must like yourself in order to like all prospects. If you show and project that you like them, then they'll like you. Get it?.

6.   Remember fun selling. The prospect is rewarding themselves and they want a positive charge from you.

– Glad you're here

– Thanks for being here.

– This is exciting.

– Gosh, I'm having fun.

– You folks have made my day.

– I sense a celebration.

– We can replace any car, but we can't replace you! Thanks for being here.

GET IT?

See? You're not in a slump, you're just not selling. <u>Start</u> <u>selling!</u> Sell yourself, sell your mind and thoughts. Have a ball. Don't forget – on your best day, you'll never meet someone you can't sell.

I believe in you. Do you?

CHAPTER TWENTY TWO

RECAP AND REVIEW

o   "I ain't in no slump, I just ain't hittin'."

o   Fundamentals.

o   Mind set – CAFÉ.

o   What's my dominant thought?

o   Am I listening or talking?

o   What about the teeth?

o   Easiest was to sell a car is not to try and sell a car, just make afriend.

CHAPTER 23

QUALITATIVE SELF-EXAMINATION

Do I have a winning mind set?

Do I get excited about going to work?

Do I have a plan?

Do I practice, drill and rehearse new techniques?

Do I try to improve specific weaknesses?

Do I work to improve communication skills?

Do I have good work habits?

Do I have a professional appearance and demeanor?

Do I greet prospects in a friendly and professional manner?

Do I investigate conversationally?

Do I present (yes, present) value in the vehicle from the customer's viewpoint?

Do I take my prospects on a _real_ demo drive?

Do I present a professional buyer's order and credit application?

Do I present the figures confidently?

Do I ask for the business – right now?

Am I a team player?

Do I have the attitude it takes to be a success?

Do I try to do the right thing?

Do I continually try to grow?

Do I go to work, to work?

Do I enjoy (really enjoy) the car business?

Am I a champion? A champion is one who can perform at the top level again and again. Never looks back. Does not dwell on the negative, but lives in the positive. Looks to grow and continually achieve new and higher accomplishments.

SEED	BENEFIT
Great greeting	Like you, comfort
Intent Statement	Professional, reduce stress, allow process
Dealership Statement	Trust, stability, here for you
Needs assessment and rapport	Servant's heart; broaden dream likes you
Price sticker (Designed to sell for)	Slows down discount, value
Trade walk-a-round	Weakens their dream
Trade statement	They're not alone; preps for pencil
Service walk	Value, comfort
Complete Buyer's Order	Professional, doing business now
Evidence Manual (upon leaving)	We're people too
Complete pencil presentation	Trust, straight forward All information, choices
Quality delivery experience	You care, friend in business, referrals
Follow-up call	Builds relationship, good survey

WHAT IS THE CUSTOMER'S PERCEPTION?

Like us

Trust us

Stable and professional

Received great value

Received great trade-in

Service

We'll be there for them

CHAPTER TWENTY THREE

RECAP AND REVIEW

o   I must be honest with myself.

o   All successful people self criticize.

o   I will be honest and fearless in my self examination.

o   I will make positive changes.

o   I am a work in progress.

CHAPTER 24

QUANTITATIVE SELF-EXAMINATION

This isn't for everyone, although it should be. It requires complete honesty. It's a reminder of one's mind set. Also, it involves straight activity management on a daily basis, And, finally, it will track your honest, self criticism of your skills in executing the sales process.

The chart is laid out with daily activity and numeric summary of your day's sales process, activity and your results.

Self Improvement Month/Year _____

Per Day Goals		Today	MTD	Today	MTD	Today	MTD	Today	MTD	Today	MTD	Today	MTD	To
	Day													
	Date													
	Attitude Today													
	Prospect Calls													
	Cards Mailed													
	Appointments Made													
%	Up's													
	Good Greeting													
	Good Rapport													
	Need Assessment													
	Veh. Presentation													
	Demo													
	Sit Down													
	Sold													
Per Day Goals	Day													
	Date													
	Attitude Today	Today	MTD	Today	MTD	Today	MTD	Today	MTD	Today	MTD	Today	MTD	To
	Prospect Calls													
	Cards Mailed													
	Appointments Made													
%	Up's													
	Good Greeting													
	Good Rapport													
	Need Assessment													
	Veh. Presentation													
	Demo													
	Sit Down													
	Sold													

1. Write down your attitude beginning the day.

2. <u>Prospect calls, cards mail</u> – You must decide up front if this is part of what you do if you want to be successful. How many appointments have you made today? Along the left hand vertical column, write in

your daily plan or you must do it for each: Prospect calls, cards mailed, appointments. Then, daily write in what you did that day.

3. The next section from Prospects Ups down through Sold is the sales process. IN the left hand vertical column write down your percentage goal on each step. It goes like this: If you talk to 10 ups, how many of that 10 can I give a quality greeting to? It better be ten out of ten if you're a professional. Next, of those 10, how many can you establish good rapport? In most cases, you should be able to establish good rapport with eight or nine.

Out of the eight prospects you've gotten this far, how many can you do an effective needs assessment and vehicle selection? Maybe 7, maybe 6. Of those, how many will you accomplish to great vehicle presentation? Maybe 5?

From the five you've got left, how many will get a great demonstration? Should be all five because they should be excited from the presentation. SO of the five left, how many can I sit down and present figures? You'll probably get four to come inside, sit down and go over figures. Then, how many did I sell?

Do this form daily and it will quantitatively point out your strengths and weaknesses. It will also show you in bright light just how critical the greeting and rapport building part of the process is.

CHAPTER TWENTY FOUR

RECAP AND REVIEW

o   I must be honest with myself.

o   Do I have a plan that I can work?

o   As I getting better (dynamic) or staying the same (static)?

o   I am a professional and I must get real.

o   I am a work in progress.

CHAPTER 25

IN CONCLUSION AND IN PROGRESS

In titling my book, I chose the word "encyclopedia." "The Encyclopedia of Selling Cars." An encyclopedia is a compilation of works and information on many subjects as well as definitive information on a special subject.

The automobile sales business is a business of many facets. I wrote "The Encyclopedia of Selling Cars" with the intent of sharing with readers facets of the sales industry that I have seen – first hand – help make people successful. I've found that success in professional sales does not come from a pill, a 1, 2, 3 step, but from a balanced approach in both life and actual sales practices.

We must have a foundation to become enormously successful. The musts are belief, purpose, desire, self-esteem and knowing we are engaged in a noble pursuit. There is no particular season for doing the "right thing."

Encyclopedias are made to be expanded. There are new thoughts and techniques that have come out even before this book makes print. Write them down. Add to your own book of knowledge and experience.

Being a part of <u>professional</u> sales is an extremely exciting work in progress. I have always been grateful to be part of it. It is all about the BBR. My hope is that "The Encyclopedia of Selling Cars" has provided help and hope to others.

My best to you,

Ted Lindsay

CPSIA information can be obtained at www.ICGtesting.com
261588BV00002BA/8/A

9 781434 311603